TEXAS ANGEL

From Loss and Love to Blessed Assurance

DO GOOD
ENTERPRISES LLC

INTENTIONAL | PURPOSEFUL | SOLUTIONS

DoGoodLeadership.me

About the Author

I am Dr. Stephanie Duguid, daughter of Margie Rector. I am a wife, mom, daughter, sister, educator, friend, and leader.

My drive to share this comes from being raised by a strong, confident woman and more than 25 years in education as a teacher and administrator. I have been a lifelong educator with degrees in Human Performance, Sports Health Care, Curriculum and Instruction, and Educational Leadership. Through all of my schooling and my life, I have had my mother as the driving force in my mind.

Now as a mom to two teenage boys that my mother never had the opportunity to meet, I strive to be a role model for them as my mother was to me! I want to be the one to show how to be strong, confident, lead by example, and serve others.

I hope you enjoy this compilation of lessons learned by reflecting on the wonderful memories and interactions with my mom. By your purchase, you are contributing to a scholarship in my mother's name as well as helping others in need.

Thank you!

Special Information

I am glad you decided to be a part of the continuation of this story and helping others through your support by purchasing. Please be sure to read the forward where I share a reflection of how this book came to be. I hope you are as touched as I was living this journey.

DO GOOD
ENTERPRISES LLC

One thing my mother always encouraged me to do was to follow my dreams. I am pursuing a personal goal of professional speaking, coaching, and training through Do Good Enterprises.

I would be honored if you would visit my website at: www.dogoodleadership.me

If you are interested in downloading a FREE Goal Setting Workbook, follow the link here: https://www.gp.dogoodleadership.me/optin

If you are interested in downloading this FREE resource highlighting 7 Simple Ways to Practice Being Present which is so important in our digital world, follow the link here: https://www.7.dogoodleadership.me/optin

Dedication

I dedicate this to my mother, Marjorie. She is my guardian angel!

Contributions/Donations

My husband and I were honored to have the opportunity to create a scholarship in my mother's memory for those pursuing a degree in education, nursing, or social work that became endowed on February 2022 on the 82nd birthday of my mother. The hope is that her memorial scholarship will help those who share her passion for education, life of giving, and supporting those in need.

Therefore, a portion of the proceeds from each eBook will be donated to her memorial scholarship at Copiah-Lincoln Community College. If you would like to donate, please do so at: Give Now - Copiah-Lincoln Community College (colin.edu)

So, THANK YOU for being a part of the everlasting legacy for my mother, my angel in heaven!

Forward

We all have someone in our life that we look up to. That may be a teacher, a friend, a family member, or even a parent. For me, it was my mom!

I have enjoyed the foundation that my mother provided. She was my mom, a teacher, a friend, a church member, and a leader in the community. She led by example and touched so many.

This book is a reflection of her life and the lessons learned. They were not written down or scripted along the way, they came about upon reflection and introspection after her passing.

I have found that certain themes have come about that were really modeled from her life, her giving, her service, and her spirit. I discovered that I have been told I honor her themes as well.

I hope you connect with the stories throughout, and the lessons learned. You will laugh, cry, feel love, and loss. But most of all, you will get a sense for what an amazing person she was.

Table of Contents

IN THE BEGINNING

A story has no beginning or end:
arbitrarily one chooses that moment
of experience from which to look
back or from which to look ahead.

~Graham Greene

Before cell phones Facebook, iTunes, or Amazon
stood a little girl with a panda bear dangling by his
ear. Sugar Land is a real place, where Imperial
Sugar was made, the Palms Theater was the towns'
gathering place, and Lakeview Elementary
appeared after driving through the perfectly
spaced and repetitive rows of a pecan tree orchard.

Source: "The old Sugar Land Refinery in Sugar Land, Texas" by
Jim Evans CC 4.0

Source: "*Palms Theater" by Cinema Treasures CC by 3.0*

Sugar Land was my hometown where I grew up in Venetian Estates on Salerno Drive with my mom and my older sister. My first strong memory is as a little girl with soft blonde hair laying gently over my ears, my eyes staring at a photographer, a small scar across the bridge of my nose from my recent break out of chicken pox, with my blue overall dress with the door flap on the front and the friendly inchworm coming out to say hello. The red and white checkered puff sleeved shirt underneath and my panda bear nearby.

These were family pictures with my mom and sister. I was smiling because had my two favorite things with me... My mom by my side and my panda bear close by.

I've always loved panda bears. They are fluffy, cuddly, grounded, consistent in their patterns, a perfect animal for a logical analytical, OCD (which should be CDO...In alphabetical order like it should be) person like me.

The National Zoo in Washington DC is where my love of panda bears began. Each year we would visit my grandmother on Northwest Connecticut Ave, and we would make a point to visit the very rare panda bears. Each trip was followed by a walk through the gift shop with yet another panda bear token bag, stuffed animal, bookmark, T-shirt, or trinket. I ended up with a whole corner of my room, shelves along the wall, and amazing memories of panda bears. I've even been told they are my spirit animal. But that explanation is for a different book ▢!

My memory of the blue dress, chicken pox scar, and panda bear is one that I'm not sure I remember from living it, or from seeing the portrait hanging on our home in Sugar Land. Either way that "vision', if you will, is the one I see the most. A recent energy centering experience explained that that particular vision is the one I hold close to my heart; my mom holding my right hand symbolizes safety and security and love, while in my left hand is the ear of my favorite panda bear, dangling in the "give me a hug" position.

I had two favorite things that I loved! One was my panda bear! My other love was my mom. Everyone has that special person in their life that is their biggest influence. The one they love, admire, and want to emulate. My mother was that person. Mom was my protector, my supporter, and my rock, always in the background as my biggest cheerleader. My mother, Marjorie, was born in 1940, in Maryland. She was the youngest of five children raised in a Christian home. She had three sisters and a brother. Her dad was in real estate but died suddenly when she was 14. Not much was shared about her dad's death. Those are her family only stories. But my mom had a strong, independent mom, I called Grammy.

Education was always a pillar in her life. Her mother was passionate about education and had a personal goal that all five of her children would attend and earn a college degree. Of the five children, all earned a bachelor's degrees and mom earned two master's degrees.

Grammy was an immigrant from the British West Indies who came to America through Ellis Island along with her 16-year-old brother. Together they had to survive and both thrived years later. Her departure from her own family at such a young age, again, was always kept a secret so it will remain a secret here too.

*** *

As the youngest of five, mom was a very loving and caring. Mommie was 25 years younger than her oldest sibling. As you can see, I called her mommie, yes, with an "ie". Not sure why, but I liked "ie" better than "y". I am a bit strong headed, which I get a little from her.

She and Grammy were very close. By the time my mom had me, two of her siblings had passed, again, not much is shared about their passing. But since I was also the youngest of the family, that was something Mommie and I had in common, we were both babies in the family which created a special bond.

I was born and raised in Texas and mom was the typical Texas woman (yet born in Maryland) .... big hair, big personality, and a big heart.

Mom was a teacher for over forty years, most of which were at John Foster Dulles High School in Stafford, Texas, teaching Government, Economics, and Leadership where her students admired her.

I vividly remember going to Dulles high school to help mom organize her classroom. The smell of the chalk dust when I drew faces on the board and the white powder all over my hands drying out my cuticles. The smell of the mimeograph pages as the ca-ching, ca-ching, ca-ching circled repeatedly making the purple ink copies that faded with greater quantities. The green grid gradebook with numbers crawling through the pages and the wideout marks dabbed throughout.

My mom loved being a teacher! She was a teacher students trusted and felt safe with. Many students who had challenges in their home, family, or other aspects of their life would seek help from her. On many occasions, she would open her home and heart to students in need. She would even "hire" her students to help her with chores around the house, yardwork, and even typing her handwritten notes so she could organize and file them. Zig Ziglar said "You never know when a moment and a few sincere words can impact a life forever", that describes my mother and her influence on others.

Mom was a great communicator and got to know her students very well. Because of her kindness and her interest in them, they openly shared highlights and challenges including terrible things like abuse, neglect, and hunger.

There was one young man who was abused on a regular basis it was even hit by a baseball bat by his dad. I remember specifically driving to his home where we picked him up. We drove up quietly with our headlights off, he quicky ran out and jumped in the car, and we drove away without being seen or heard. We didn't find out much about the details, but he lived in our guest room for several months until he graduated from Dulles and found a job where he could support himself and live on his own.

***

We also had a surprise exchange student from Germany named Antja whose first host family was not very nice to her. She moved in with us and taught me the German alphabet and sometimes forgot she was in America. In the German culture it was common to go outside topless. One day she was sunning in our backyard following her German culture, topless, and our poor elderly neighbor almost had a heart attack. He was very frazzled when he called my mom and said that he just couldn't go in his backyard. When my mother asked why, he said we had a naked girl in the backyard, and he just couldn't go outside! Antja finished her exchange year living at our house, with her clothes on, until she returned to Germany. A few years later we had the opportunity to visit her in Germany while we went on a church choir tour and had lunch at a McDonald's. It was *JUST* like the American McDonalds, well almost. Their fish sandwich was actually cod.

***

Mom always opened her heart and her home to help others in need. Mom was a lot of great things. But one thing she was not, was "on time". Mom was late for everything!!!! She was late for work every day. She was late for church, late for parties, late for games, late for dinner. She was always late. The funny thing is, she tried to trick herself into being on time by adjusting the time on every clock in the house to read as if they were 15 minutes ahead. That still didn't work. Thank goodness cell phones weren't invented yet because those are set automatically! Most people who are late feel bad about it or those hosting the event get offended when you are late. But mom referred it to being "fashionably late" so she could make an entrance. In most cases it worked! We always had a running joke that she would be late to her own funeral.

***

Mom would continue to honor her beliefs by living a life of service and giving to others. Mom was very active in the Old Saints Episcopal Church on Dulles Ave which happened to be across the street from Dulles High School. She was a female lay reader and Chalise bearer and was very involved in the congregation, Sunday school, choir, and outreach activities. We spent most of our Sunday mornings every week at the church preparing for both services and joining in with the choir for the second service. One day in particular mom and the others church service leaders were preparing for a large number of worshippers in the congregation due to a special program being presented. In fact they prepared two Chalices for this particular Sunday. However not many came that Sunday due to weather, so they grossly overprepared. At the end of the service, there was an exceptional amount of wine left in the Chalices. In fact, only part of one was consumed. And in the Episcopal Church, you are not allowed to discard the remaining wine down the drain once it has been blessed, you must consume it. Mom and one other had to consume the entire chalice and a half of wine... yes wine, not grape juice. That was when I found out my mom was a lightweight. Yes, mom got drunk at church drinking the leftover wine from the service. Although I was 14, I did drive home. I had experience from driving on the ranch. It was much safer that way, trust me!

***

My mother spent her days and nights dedicated to her family, students, church, and the community. She had two daughters, Kimberly, and me, Stephanie, that were the center of her life, but also considered her students her "kids". She started teaching in the 1960's where she not only taught the curriculum of her courses, but also life skills, problem solving, critical thinking, all while demonstrating optimism, strength, and positivity through her caring nature. Her Christian demeanor and open heart spilled over into her classrooms.

Before the "digital age" of computers, cell phones, and the internet, mom was the community "Welcome Wagon Lady".

Welcome Wagon Graduation 1974

If you've never heard about Welcome Wagon, their mission and goals, please enjoy an excerpt from WelcomeWagon.com in the History section

Welcome Wagon ® was founded in 1928 by an insightful marketing man in Memphis, Tennessee, Thomas Briggs. Mr. Briggs was inspired by stories of early Conestoga "welcome wagons" that would meet and greet westward travelers, providing fresh food and water for the journey. He created Welcome Wagon ® to embody this same spirit of warm hospitality and welcome. He hired "hostesses", women who were friendly and knowledgeable about their neighborhood, to personally deliver baskets of gifts supplied y local businesses to new homeowners.

Over a cup of coffee, hostesses would tell their new mover all about their community while handing out gits and coupons from local businesses. This hostess network expanded across the country until, aside from Briggs, and just a handful of males, Welcome Wagon ® become one of the first all-female companies I the United States.

https://welcomewagon.com/history

Welcome Wagon

NO HAPPY HELLO is ever quite equal to the warm welcome extended to families who move, by the Welcome Wagon Hostess . . . complete with a galaxy of gifts and helpful information on shopping and community facilities.
In Toronto call
WELCOME WAGON LIMITED–364-5429

Source: Toronto Life, *November 1969*

Mommie was Sugar Land's Welcome Wagon Lady. She was the one in the community that would go to a new community member's home with her very flowery yellow wicker basket of goodies,

"Welcoming" them to the town, share key aspects of the community, and give them a few gifts. She would then share her information to be the go-to person for any questions. She knew how to build relationships and interact with others.

LESSON 1: BE PRESENT

Life gives you plenty of time to do whatever you want to do if you stay in the present moment

~Deepak Chopra

Throughout my life my mom was there. Not just around, but there! Physically present. When I saw her, she always gave me a warm embracing hug where I felt loved, she looked me in the eyes and had a genuine caring gaze as she asked me questions and listen to my responses. She was present! Mom was really present! Proof of her presence is found in the thousands of pictures she was in.

This was before cell phones and digital cameras where you could quickly check and see the image in seconds. This was when you had to take pictures with an actual camera, wind the film, maybe even attach the bulb at the top with the flash that was only good for four photo attempts. When you had to take the spent film to the drug store called Eckerd's in Sugarland or the small box in the middle of the parking lot called Fotomat.

Source: "A Fotomat kiosk in Massachusetts in 1987", by unknown CC BY-SA 3.0

There you picked up an envelope, selected your choice of prints, added your personal info, licked the envelope to securely close it, and trustingly give them to a stranger, or put it in the drop box. Then a week later you had to make intentional plans to pick them up and hope you were able to get a great picture.

We had thousands of pictures around the house. Drawers, and wall collages that were framed, photo books, and more shoe boxes.

Mom was everywhere. My volleyball pictures, in her classroom, smiling with friends at my best friend's wedding (in official pictures with the wedding party), holding flowers, next to plants, holding balloons, anything she saw beauty in she took a picture with it. I used to roll my eyes each time she pulled the camera out but now it provides such amazing memories.

When my mom died, I initially struggled with her loss. I didn't know why she was taken, and I wanted her back. I was being selfish because I kept saying "I". But she was my mommie and she was a loving force of nature.

LESSON 2: KNOW YOUR WHY

When we lose someone we love, we must learn not to live without them, but to live with the love and left behind.

~Unknown

When I read that quote, I suddenly realized, my mom wasn't completely gone. She left a blazing path of love behind. And really, I am thinking in a small manner, she left a legacy to me, my sister, and to everyone she encountered. Although it was not clear to me when she was physically here, now I know her *WHY* in life. She lived to bring the best out in others, she looked to support and help others, and she lived to FIND THE GOOD in others. That was her *WHY*. It is evident in every memory!

When I reflect on my *WHY* I feel I'm doing the same thing. Although, as a kid I was merely going through the motions following what my mom did but now I realize she is a part of me. I tried to resist going into get into education but was drawn into the profession non-traditionally. I went to school to become an athletic trainer and later had an offer to substitute an eighth-grade math class for a long-term contract. Here we go! I went back to school for a postbaccalaureate teacher certification and a second masters. I was a teacher. And mom knew that was my profession.

On my third day of teaching at my first teaching job, flowers arrived in my classroom. They were beautiful, colorful, made me smile, and had a note from mom. The card said, "I am proud of you! Love Mom!" It was on the third day of teaching as the long-term sub that I received the late-night call about the accident. The call came from a hospital in Tyler, Texas. I immediately thought they had the wrong number. What was my mother doing in Tyler, Texas? That was four hours away from Sugar Land. How can she be in critical care, and they are asking me for her medical directives? Do they have the correct person? While I was on the phone, they said she coded. And they did confirm it was her. I never got to thank her! She was gone!

On August 23, 2001, at 12:26AM, my mother was in a fatal single car accident. She was 61 years old.

***

Over the next year, my husband and I taught at the same schools teaching the same grades and had common students. Yes, he succumbed to education as an English teacher, and I was a math and science teacher. We taught 7th through 12th grades and had this amazing report with all students even those that other teachers had daily problems with. Not the Duguid's!

Before mom died, we talked about the possibility of furthering my education and getting a doctorate. I loved going to school! I always said and still do, that if I would get paid to go to school, I would do that as my career in a heartbeat. But unfortunately, my current student loans that I have been paying for since deferment ended in 2006 would prove otherwise.

Therefore, as soon as she died, I was on a mission to get my doctorate as soon as I possibly could to fulfill my promise. I enrolled immediately after finishing my second masters in the fall of 2003. My goal was to finish in the minimum three years period. I graduated as Dr. Stephanie Duguid in January 2006.

***

When mom died, she did so outside of Tyler, Texas. At that time, I was in Phoenix, Arizona, and my sister was in San Francisco, California, while mom's home was in Sugar Land, Texas and she wished to be buried in North Carolina at the Salem Church next to her own mother in the family plot. To say there was some planning, traveling, and timing was an understatement. The logistics alone were challenging! My sister and I had to get to Texas. We had to get mom from Tyler, Texas, to Sugar Land. We had to arrange her cremation, a funeral in Texas and transportation along with a small family service in North Carolina. We had to time it so that we could travel **with her** from Texas to North Carolina and our only option at that time was through Dallas. Our layover in Dallas proved to be even more of a challenge when our flights were cancelled. They couldn't get a flight until the next day to North Carolina due to weather. The funny thing about all of this was that mom *WAS* late to her own funeral! All we could do is laugh!!!!

At the family funeral I announced I had followed in mom's footsteps and was a teacher. My cousins beamed with pride. They told me she would be so proud of me! At that time, I could feel her presence and knew she approved.

LESSON 3: INTROSPECTION AND REFELCTION

Reflection. Looking back so that the view looking forward is even clearer.

~ Unknown

Mom died on August 23, 2001, on an isolated road outside Tyler, Texas. And since Arizona, California, Texas, and North Carolina were all part of a very complex equation for her final plans, we knew it would be a challenge. We had to navigate the planning, travel, service, emotions, and the many questions. My question was why? I was 27 years old, and my mom died in a single car accident all alone because she fell asleep. Why didn't she stay the night at her friend's house? She was ejected because she would not wear a seat belt. Why? Of course, I continued to review the past events and say, "if only she…" and fill in the blank. Or "she should have…" and fill in the blank again.

Although they say hindsight is 2020, she was already gone. There was nothing I could say or do to change the present reality. But still, why? My mom was a Christian woman, went to and served at church, was a teacher and friend to thousands of students, served in the community, and was MY mom.

So out of all the people in the world, why was my mom the one that died? She was making a difference in the lives of others and in mine. I struggled with her loss. I was a teacher because of her. So, every day when I went to work, I thought of her. When I thought about going back to school to further my education, I thought of her. When I *tried* to cook (HAHA), I thought of her. When songs came on the radio, I thought of her. *SO WHY*?

 I was devastated but soon understood and felt peace with why she was taken two weeks later. Do you remember what happened then?

***

On September 11, 2001, close to 3000 individuals perished in the terrorist attacks in New York, Pennsylvania, and Washington D.C. On September 11, 2001, terrorists took over four American Airline airplanes and crashed two into the World Trade Towers in New York, one at the Pentagon in Washington D.C., and one ended up in a field in Pennsylvania. On September 11, 2001, the world stopped in awe with the attacks on America. That day thousands lost their lives. Their families' children, friends, and others loved ones will all be asking the same question I did…. WHY?

Although that event is the worst attack with unexplainable and horrific result and effects, I finally understood why my mom was gone. My mom, with her smiling face, bright colored lipstick, big hair, high heels, flowers all around, big personality, Texas mom, the Welcome Wagon Lady, was needed! God needed her! She was the one to welcome all those mom's, dad's, friends, and loved ones, lost in the events of 9/11 to heaven. She is in her element as the "heavenly hostess". Although it may sound strange, I'm now at peace with her loss.

LESSON 4: FIND THE GOOD

Everyday may not be good, but there is something good in every day!

~Unknown

In the days, weeks, months, and years ahead there were struggles, more questions, sadness, and moments of elation. But in every situation, I didn't want to be the one that made excuses, complained, or blamed others. I decided to live life to the fullest and make her proud. I decided to *FIND THE GOOD* in everything. I'm sure you may have rolled your eyes saying "Great, another Pollyanna! She is going to pretend everything is good to avoid the real stuff going on." No! That is not it at all.

We always hear that "everything happens for a reason". We just have to *FIND THE GOOD* in everything. We need to find a positive light rather than dwell on the negative. The area we focus on is the area that will grow. Positive breeds positive, and negative breeds negative. I choose positive!

In my life, I choose to *FIND THE GOOD*. Let's explore this with a few word pairs to help with the mind shift.

- Half empty or half full?
- Problem or opportunity?
- Have to or get to?
- I am short or I am vertically challenged?
- I can't or how can I?
- NOW YOU TRY....

Let me give you a couple of some examples.

I lost my keys in my office. In order to find them, I had to clean up my desk, put away files, and go through some lingering mail, while rearranging the desktop. I found my keys! But better yet, I also had the opportunity to clean my desk. FIND THE GOOD!

This is a personal one. A few years ago, I came to a crossroads....I was offered my dream job, an upper administrative position. But I would be required to move which would take me away from my kids, husband, and a lot more. Now, let me remind you, I have a loving husband that works with me, and, at the time, two boys in elementary school that are my world, and they LOVE their school, and their mom. Now, I was at a crossroads....do I take the job that I WANT and make my family move, or do I decline the job and feel like I am "settling" for what I am doing now.

What would you do?

I decided to forgo the professional opportunity (That other felt I SHOULD take) and choose my kids while following my heart. I wanted to EMPOWER myself and put my family first. I decided to be selfless rather than selfish! I decided to forge my own path utilizing my skills and experience in another manner. Now I do not feel like I am going through the motions of my job, I feel like I can do anything and am now in control of my future! *FIND THE GOOD.*

***

With mom, although I'm still very sad for her loss and I miss her terribly, I know she was needed more in heaven. I also know she's watching over me and is my guardian Angel. I truly believe that in my daily life. Things I see remind me of her! Everything from sounds, scents like her Red by Giorgio Beverly Hills perfume, certain flowers, songs, and phrases. I had always thought and believed she was around, but that was my own mind believing it. However, she vehemently validated her presence several years later.

***

Fast forward to August 16, 2009, when my second son Dalton was born. At his birth on Sunday, he was a healthy baby and even had an excellent well-baby visit at the end of the week on Friday. On Saturday, August 22nd, he stopped breathing at home, started turning blue, and had a full body red rash. My husband and I rushed him to the Baptist Hospital, where he was born, but it was not looking good. The medical staff was challenged to keep him alert and engaged. They were not equipped to care for a newborn. He needed to be transferred to the Pediatric ER at University of Mississippi Medical Center down the street. As new Mississippi residents, we didn't know about the pediatric ER and automatically brought him to Baptist. Luckily, the attending physician knew Dalton was in trouble and had a resident travel with Dalton in the ambulance when he was transferred to a second hospital. Fortunately, Dalton was a direct admit since he arrived by ambulance. Unfortunately, we were not allowed to see him until the medical staff was able to get him stabilized and fill out all the paperwork. I was not a happy parent at this time! Once admitted he was sedated, intubated, had a spinal tap done, dozens of tests, and in short, there was not a reasonable answer for his lack of breathing or his rash, and the prognosis for his condition was not positive.

At around midnight, Dalton was transferred to the pediatric Intensive Care Unit (ICU). While my husband and I were in the ICU waiting room, we were both very emotional to say the least. I happened to glance at the clock and could not believe what I saw! **It was 12:26AM on August**

23rd, the same date and time my mother passed away 8 years prior. At that very moment, I knew that my mother was with us and prayed that she could help my son. Although there were many unknowns, I felt that he would be OK! I had always trusted her, more now than ever, even though she was not physically here.

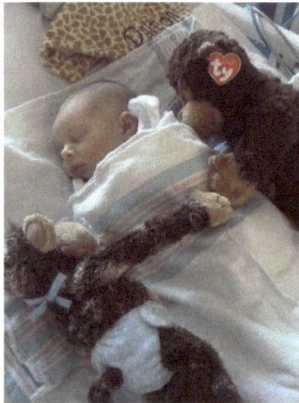

Dalton was in the hospital for nine days and was a patient in the Intensive Care Unit, Transition Care Unit, and on the Pediatric Floor. Through his stay, he developed a blood clot in his left leg at the point of entry of his central line, had a focal seizure, and many other challenges. Our first few months of his life consisted of multiple trips to see his hematologist, neurologist, infectious disease doctor, and of course his pediatrician. And after all the visits, all the challenges, all the concerns, Dalton is truly a miracle. I honestly believe my mother had something to do with that!

***

In 2012, eleven years after mom's passing, we decided to take a road trip to visit her grave site. We planned a trip to go from Mississippi, through Tennessee, over to North Carolina, and back through South Carolina and the southern states to return to Mississippi. On the way, I knew that mom was at the Salem Church Cemetery in North Carolina. We put it into GPS and went on our trip.

As we were getting closer to the cemetery, I wanted to pick up some flowers. We stopped at a local store to get a bouquet of her favorites! GPS took us straight to the Salem Church, but something was off. I don't remember the church looking like this. I don't remember the cemetery on that side of the sanctuary. I don't remember it being this close to the road! I don't remember it because it was the WRONG CHURCH! We did a quick search (now this was before the awesome Google we have now) and there were 17 Salem Churches in the local area. We had gone to the wrong place! All we could do was laugh. And I know mom was laughing too!

We stopped to grab a bite to eat and searched the cemetery locator. We FOUND HER! She was three hours east at another Salem Church. We drove three more hours, found a hotel for the night, and planned to see her in the morning.

The next morning, I was a bit emotional. We were FINALLY going to see mom again after 11 years. I had never seen her headstone. My boys had never met her. We arrived at the church, and it looked more like what I remembered. Thanks goodness! I found the cemetery but had a hard time finding her! I walked around for about 10 minutes and there it was. Her beautiful headstone with angels on the corners. Her stone reads, "She touched and enlightened the lives of many". Yes, she did! On that day my boys got to meet their grandmother. On that day, I was able to find my mommie. On that day I was able to say thank you for watching over my son Dalton in his time of need. On that day...

Today, my son is 13 years old and has so many characteristics of my mother. He has a big personality and a big heart. He even says and does things that she would say and do when I was a child, and he has NEVER met her! He is empathetic, caring, has confidence, and loves hugs! Talk about connections. Dalton even talks about her as if he has met her. Many say he is a child of God because of all of his health challenges in his first days of life! He survived and even thrived.   He has mom's personality, her humor, her smile, and her caring nature. He has a connection to those around him and especially the older population. He just cares about people!

LESSON 5: BE A SERVANT LEADER

I've learned that people will forget what you said, people will forget what you did, but people will never forget how you made them feel.

~Maya Angelou

Mom was a teacher for more than 40 years. When you said Mrs. Rector in our community, you automatically thought of Dulles High school. Mom taught government, economics, and leadership and she was the favorite teacher of most. She would come to class late almost every day (due to taking me to school and the domino effect of morning schedules). She would walk in with her colorful dress, high heels, big smile, big hair, big personality, and bright lipstick. She commanded her classroom. She knew her students. She listened, interacted, and talked to them respectfully, inside and outside the classroom. Student loved her.

I remember so many times when we would be out and about, we would run into current or former students that would eagerly come up to us and yell, "Mrs. Rector!" She would immediately turn around and her face would light up. Then she would call them by name and continue with a full conversation like they were best friends. Now you saw I said she would call their name. That didn't happen with only her current students. That was ALL students. Even the ones from years ago! That happened in Sugar Land, Houston, Austin, San Antonio, Colorado, Maryland, and even happen more than once in Washington D.C.! It happened everywhere we went. Everyone connected to her, and she made them feel special, important, and unique. She made me feel that way too. She was definitely a servant leader. One that led by example. She wasn't a leader at the school by position, but by her interaction with others. Her form of leadership was not only present in school but at church and in the community. As I mentioned before she was involved in church as the Chalice bear and a lay reader. But also involved in the choir too and the outreach programs like Habitat for Humanity. She simply loved to help others.

***

When I think of my mom, I remember so many things, positive and negative, good and bad. But I make a point to *FIND THE GOOD*. Was it all roses all the time? Absolutely not! We had our differences, our challenges, and varying opinions. But overall, I had an amazing model of for a mom. She loved unconditionally, she led purely, she was my protector, and she was my rock.

So, in your life, no matter where you are or what you're experiencing, I encourage you to *FIND THE GOOD!*

SUMMARY: LESSONS LEARNED

After the rain, the sun will appear.
There is life. After the pain, the joy
will still be here.

~ Walt Disney

My mother has been gone for over 20 years as of the writing of this message. She has been present for me on many occasions, but especially with the health scare with my son. I think and feel my mother every day! She is truly my guardian angel.

I saw how she impacted those around her through a life of service in education, the church, and in the community. **My mother dedicated her entire life to adding value to others.**

Let's talk seriously for a minute…. we all have come here to this particular space at this time for a reason. We are looking for that light, the inspiration, the motivation, the connection, the

WOW factor. I cannot say or do anything to make you change or to *FIND THE GOOD*...you have to WANT to do that yourself...but I can guide you! Know there is a reason you chose this book. There is a reason you are reading these words. There is a reason you are here at this very moment.

In my 27 years of life I had with my mom on this Earth, she taught me many lessons. And although I didn't realize it when she was here, I realized it when I think of her through reflection. I had to cope with losing her. But through the love I had for her, my husband, and my children, I realize she is always here.

Assurance means to be confident in mind or manner, or something that inspires or tends to inspire confidence. Blessed means worthy of adoration, bringing happiness and thankfulness. Put them together and Blessed Assurance is inspirational confidence leading to happiness and thankfulness.

The connections I feel with my mother through my thoughts, memories, actions, my son's interactions, and stories from those around me prove that I am experiencing Blessed Assurance through the confidence and happiness I feel knowing my mother is here! And no, she is not physically here. She is here in my thoughts, my actions, my memories, and my opportunities.

After the loss and understanding my own personal ways I became at peace with her untimely death, I understood her purpose. All the dots became connected. She set a wonderful example for us all. If we all could do these five things throughout our lives, we would be whole, we would be a role model for others, we would be content.

1. Be Present
2. Know Your Why
3. Introspection and Reflection
4. FIND THE GOOD
5. Be a Servant Leader

I know my mom is here. I can sense it in my son, in my profession, and in my daily life. Thank you for demonstrating Blessed Assurance!

***

Thank you for taking time to read this book. It is a combination of memories and lessons learned. Although I didn't realize it at the time, my mother was also my teacher while being my mom, demonstrating her why. She was showing me how to be present, learning to reflect, always trying to FIND THE GOOD, and being a servant leader through her daily actions. Through the loss of my mom, the love I have for my family, and the unique validating experiences since her loss, I truly embraced her Blessed Assurance!

Thank you, Mom!

WHAT'S NEXT?

1. Read my next book, *Texas Angel: Part 2*
2. Pick up the compilation of more than 800 family and friend recipes, *Recipes from a Texas Angel in Heaven*.
3. If you are interested in life coaching, let's connect!
4. If you are looking for a speaker for an event to share a program on communication, connection, positive leadership, or change, let's connect (see page 66)
5. If you are a mom and a leader and want to become more confident and lead with intentionality and purpose, reach out on Facebook or on my website! I would love to connect! www.DoGoodLeadership.me

One thing my mother always encouraged me to do was to follow my dreams. I am pursuing a personal goal of professional speaking, coaching, and training through Do Good Enterprises.

I would be honored if you would visit my website at: www.dogoodleadership.me

Dr. Stephanie Duguid

DO GOOD ENTERPRISES LLC

- /DoGoodLeadership
- /stephanie-duguid
- /dogoodenterprises/
- /drsduguid

As a lifetime educator, health and wellness specialist, and avid speaker, coach, and leader, I am excited to be a part of your journey as a catalyst for positive change. I hope you enjoy motivational moments, positive outlooks, empowering and engaging opportunities, and health transformations. I look forward to working with you through Intentional | Purposeful | Solutions at Do Good Enterprises, LLC.

TALKING POINTS

- Being a catalyst for positive change
- The power of positive leadership
- Why perspective matters
- Connecting through communication

www.DoGoodLeadership.me

If you are interested in downloading a FREE Goal Setting Workbook, follow the link here: https://www.gp.dogoodleadership.me/optin

If you are interested in downloading this FREE resource highlighting 7 Simple Ways to Practice Being Present which is so important in our digital world, follow the link here: https://www.7.dogoodleadership.me/optin

Thank you for taking time to read *Texas Angel Part 1*.

Be sure to look for additional titles by Dr Stephanie Duguid on Amazon or visit

www.dogoodleadership.me.